BOB DOLE

A Pictorial
Biography of a
Kansan

Printed in the United States of America by Rand Graphics, Inc., Wichita, Kan.

ISBN 1-880652-87-0

Library of Congress Catalog Number 96-060997

Bob Dole: A Pictorial Biography of a Kansan is published by the Books Division of The Wichita Eagle and Beacon Publishing Co.

PHOTO CREDITS

Cover portrait by Joel Sartore

The Wichita Eagle — Pages 8 (Jeff Tuttle), 55 (bottom), 56 (bottom), 57 (top), 58 (bottom), 61 (clipping), 62 (bottom), 63, 64 (clipping), 65 (left), 66 (bottom), 67, 68, 69 (top), 70 (left), 72 (bottom left), 73 (clipping), 74, 76 (clipping), 77 (clipping), 78 (bottom photo, clipping), 79 (bottom), 80 and 81 (Mike Hutmacher), 82, 84, 85 (Joel Sartore), 86 (bottom), 87 (top), 89 (Tuttle), 92 (Richard Hernandez), 93 (clipping), 95 (Brian Corn), 96 (Ken Mantyla), 98 (photo, Hutmacher), 99 (Hutmacher), 101 (Hutmacher), 102 (Craig Hacker).

We are grateful to the following individuals and institutions for contributing their photographs and mementos for this book.

The Dole family, courtesy of Gloria Nelson and Norma Jean Steele —

Pages 10, 11, 12, 13, 14, 15, 16, 17, 18, 19, 21 (top), 22, 23 (top), 24 (photo), 26 (bottom), 28, 31 (left), 33, 34, 35 (photo), 36, 37 (bottom), 38, 39, 42, 43, 44, 45 (top), 49 (top), 50 (bottom), 51, 52 (bottom), 53, 54, 56 (top), 60 (right), 62 (top), 65 (right), 76 (top), 79 (top), 86 (top), 100.

The Russell News/Record — Pages 20, 23 (bottom), 25 (bottom), 26 (top), 27 (photo), 29, 30 (top), 37 (top), 46, 47, 48 (top), 49 (bottom), 52 (top), 55 (top), 60 (left), 64 (photos), 69 (bottom), 70 (right), 71, 72 (top, bottom right), 75, 76 (bottom), 77 (top), 78 (top), 103 (top).

The Associated Press — Pages 57 (bottom), 58 (top), 59, 61 (left), 73 (photo), 86 (left), 87 (bottom), 90 (bottom), 93 (bottom), 97 (top), 105, 108, 109, 110, 111.

Dole Senate Office — Pages 88, 90 (top, center), 91, 94, 97 (bottom), 103 (bottom)

Washburn University — Pages 40, 41

University of Kansas — Pages 30 (bottom), 31 (bottom)

Hays Daily News — Page 83 (Charlie Riedel)

Russell Public Library — Pages 32, 35, 48, 52, 66 (clippings)

Russell High School — Pages 24, 27 (clippings)

Ralph Resley — Pages 21 (bottom), 104

G.B. "Bub" Dawson — Page 45 (bottom)

Adolph Reisig — Page 25 (top)

Russell County Historical Museum — Page 98 (bottom)

CONTENTS

Acknowledgments   4

Introduction   6

Bob Dole: A Look Back   9

LIFE IN RUSSELL, KANSAS   10

SERVING HIS COUNTRY   32

EARLY POLITICS   46

WASHINGTON   52

"THE WHITE HOUSE OR HOME" 105

Acknowledgments

Bob Dole has devoted his adult life to public service,
much of it well documented in words and photographs.
This book, however, starts on the plains of Russell, Kansas,
and captures Dole's life as a youngster; as a popular and
athletic teenager; as a soldier grievously wounded
in World War II; as a young county attorney and
state legislator — all before his extraordinary rise to
leadership of the U.S. Senate's majority party, and his
1996 quest for the presidency.

A book of this nature, composed of photographs
and material both current and decades old, is an
expression of the hard work and generous spirit of many
people. Family and friends who have known Dole longest
and best have offered their assistance in full measure,
graciously sharing their memories and
photographic treasures.

Thanks first should be offered to Dole's sisters,
Gloria Nelson and Norma Jean Steele, for their boundless
efforts to make this record thorough. They opened
the doors to their family homes, sharing their memories
and providing most of the early images on these pages.
Our appreciation extends not only for their contributions
to this book, but for their helpfulness and hospitality
through the years. They, their late brother, Kenneth, and
their parents, Doran and Bina Dole, unfailingly
demonstrated their Kansas spirit with their openness and
their welcoming of strangers into their homes.

We also express our deepest appreciation to
Russell Townsley, former editor and publisher of the
Russell Daily News. In addition to his great assistance on

this book, Mr. Townsley always donated generous amounts of time to answer inquiries over the years, when media from around the world camped on his doorstep. Probably no one outside the family has known Bob Dole better than he.

We offer thanks also to Allan Evans, current editor and publisher of the Russell News/Record, who worked with Mr. Townsley for more than 40 years. Mr. Evans' help in locating photos and stories was invaluable.

Marcie Adler, a Russell native and longtime aide to Sen. Dole, generously offered her counsel, opened doors in Washington and unearthed photos. Her great assistance, coming during the hectic weeks before and immediately after Dole's resignation from the Senate, is testament to Ms. Adler's energy, pride and commitment to sharing the Bob Dole story.

There is a long list of other Kansans who have allowed us to probe their memories for this book. Among those who deserve special mention, however, are Dean Banker, third-generation clothier in Russell who tucks a bit of good humor into every purchase leaving his store; Adolph Reisig and Ralph Resley, both Russell High School classmates and teammates of Bob Dole; G.B. "Bub" Dawson, whose family owned the drugstore where teenager Dole worked at the soda fountain; faculty and staff of Russell High School; and Patti Slider, director of development at the Washburn University School of Law.

To these and the numerous others who graciously offered their assistance, we offer our thanks.

INTRODUCTION

Long before German gunfire in World War II altered his career choices, Bob Dole learned that working longer and harder than anyone else increased his chances of success. This small-town America work ethic has guided Dole throughout a 46-year-long political career unequaled by any other Kansan.

Dole has matched a bulldog ambition with a fierce sense of competitiveness, some might even say combativeness. These twin drives lifted him from the windswept streets of Russell, Kansas, to the leadership of the United States Senate.

Still, one towering pinnacle has defied his unceasing quest for leadership — the presidency of the United States. Not that he hasn't tried. His 1996 attempt marks a third assault upon the perilous slopes of presidential politics, all the more remarkable because lesser beings tend to fall from stardom after a single failed attempt.

Whenever Dole is knocked down, he rises again, seemingly gaining strength from adversity. When he failed to win his party's presidential nomination in 1980 and 1988, he picked himself up, dusted himself off and looked back on those setbacks as mere learning experiences. They only made him strive harder.

Only two other Kansas Republicans have been awarded their party's presidential nomination. Alfred Mossman Landon served two terms as governor before he won the nomination in 1936. He lost the election to President Franklin D. Roosevelt. Dwight David Eisenhower sprang from a boyhood in Abilene, Kansas, into a spectacular military career that won him the presidency in 1952 and 1956.

But Landon was a transplant from Ohio, and Eisenhower's family moved to Kansas from Texas when the future president was 1 year old. Should Dole succeed, he would be the first native Kansan to occupy the White House.

As Senate majority leader, Dole sat as close to the throne of power as just about anyone gets in Washington, discounting the heartbeat-away element

of the vice presidency. He once described the power of his office to marshal political might behind vital issues that can affect people's lives around the globe as "beyond my wildest dreams and fantasies."

Dole had not dreamed of entering politics when he was a kid growing up in Russell. His high school years were filled with activities straight out of Norman Rockwell paintings — lettering in football, basketball and track, delivering newspapers, jerking sodas at a local drugstore and scooping wheat at the grain elevator his father managed. Drugstore contacts inspired him to become a pre-med student at the University of Kansas, but his interest focused on sports.

The guns of war in Europe and the Pacific lured him from the campus into the Army with its new opportunities for leadership. Several training camps later, 2nd Lt. Dole was sent to Italy and assigned to the 10th Mountain Division. His platoon, assigned to reclaim Hill 913 near Bologna, came under withering fire from German defenders.

Dole went down, his right shoulder shattered and his arms and legs paralyzed for a time. He spent most of the next 3 years in hospitals before recovering to the point he could think once again of college. His useless right arm ruled out a medical or sports career, so he chose to earn a law degree instead.

He won a seat in the Kansas Legislature in 1950 while still in law school. That was followed by four terms as Russell County attorney, and when a congressional opening beckoned in 1960, Dole went running. His romance with Washington politics had begun.

Dole, faithful to his conservative home district, spent relatively quiet years in the House, but that changed dramatically after a Senate seat opened in Kansas in 1968. Dole moved swiftly to fill the vacancy and became a key spokesman and motivator for the GOP minority, especially with a Republican — President Richard Nixon — now in the White House.

With his willingness to work longer and harder than anyone else, Dole periodically filled two demanding jobs simultaneously. In 1971, Nixon chose him for GOP national chairman, partly as a reward for his unflagging defense of administration policies. Dole's loyalty to Nixon continued as the Watergate scandal unfolded, and was a factor — in addition to Republican difficulties in general and a particularly tough opponent — in the closeness of his 1974 re-election.

President Gerald Ford turned to Dole as his vice presidential running mate in 1976. Dole took on the role of point man in countering the Carter-Mondale platform. He would later quip, "I went for the jugular — my own," but he conceded that the loss and criticism of his role in the campaign had "a sobering impact."

After his quickly aborted presidential campaign in 1980, Dole again devoted his full energies to his expanding role of leadership in the U.S. Senate. When the 1984 elections gave Republicans continued control of the Senate, Dole's colleagues voted him majority leader. He served continuously as leader of the Senate's Republicans for more than 11 years, longer than anyone else.

Dole suffered deeply after his second presidential bid failed in 1988. But only briefly. He quickly remounted his leadership podium and went to bat for the Bush-Quayle ticket and other Republican candidates around the country, storing up valuable credits for his eventual success in the 1996 presidential primaries.

He had worked tirelessly in the Senate to achieve consensus on dozens of major issues, earning the respect of his GOP friends and former Democratic foes alike.

Upon his resignation, his Senate colleagues offered moving tributes. Some focused on his background and personal traits, others on his legislative record. From both sides of the aisle, however, came praise for Dole's leadership.

Many referred to him as being among the giants in U.S. Senate history.

Dole's farewell speech was marked by his characteristic humor, anecdotes and references to current and former colleagues, and a quotation from his hero, World War II supreme commander and fellow Kansan, President Dwight Eisenhower:

" 'As we peer into society's future, we – you and I – and our government – must avoid the impulse to live only for today, plundering for our own ease and convenience, the precious resources of tomorrow.

" 'We cannot mortgage the material assets of our grandchildren without risking the loss of their political and spiritual heritage. We want democracy to survive for all the generations to come, not to become the insolvent phantom of tomorrow.'

"I think those words are just as good today as they were 35 years ago when President Eisenhower spoke them. We can lead or we can mislead as the people's representatives, but whatever we do, we will be held responsible. We are going to be held responsible and accountable. I am not talking about 1996. I am talking about any time over the next century.

"So, the Bible tells us that to everything there is a season, and I think my season in the Senate is about to come to an end. But the new season makes this moment far less the closing of one chapter than the opening of another. We all take pride in the past, but we all live for the future.

"I agree with prairie poet Carl Sandburg, who told us:

Yesterday is a wind gone down,
a sun dropped in the West.
I tell you there is nothing in the world
only an ocean of tomorrows,
a sky of tomorrows.

"Like everybody here, I am an optimist. I believe our best tomorrows are yet to be lived. So I, again, thank you.

"God bless America, and God bless the U.S. Senate."

The following pages offer a glimpse into the life of this extraordinary Kansan, looking at where he came from, where he has been and, possibly, where he is headed.

BOB DOLE: A LOOK BACK

July 22, 1923: Robert Dole is born in Russell to parents Doran and Bina Dole.

June 1941: Graduates from Russell High School; letters in three sports.

August 1941: Enrolls at University of Kansas as pre-med student.

December 1944: Ships overseas and prepares to fight Germans in Italy.

June 1943: Enters the Army; later attends Officer Candidate School.

1948: Marries Phyllis Holden.
1949: Enrolls at Washburn University.

April 1945: Severely wounded in attack on Hill 913.
1945-1948: Recovers in stateside hospitals.

1950: Elected to the Kansas Legislature.

1952: Graduates from Washburn with law degree; elected Russell County attorney.

1954: Daughter, Robin, born; re-elected county attorney.

1956: Re-elected county attorney.

1958: Re-elected county attorney.

1960: Elected to first term in U.S. House of Representatives.

1962: Re-elected to Congress.

1964: Re-elected to Congress.

1966: Re-elected to Congress.

1968: Elected to the U.S. Senate.

1972: Divorced from Phyllis Holden.

1971: Named GOP national chairman.

1973: Replaced as GOP national chairman.

1975: Marries Elizabeth Hanford of North Carolina.

1974: Re-elected to U.S. Senate by narrow margin.

1976: Chosen as President Ford's running mate.

1979: Announces first bid for GOP presidential nomination.

1980: Withdraws from GOP presidential race; re-elected to Senate.

1981: Becomes chairman of Senate Finance Committee.

1984: Elected Senate majority leader.

1987: Announces second bid for GOP presidential nomination.

1986: Re-elected to U.S. Senate; elected Senate minority leader.

1988: Withdraws from presidential race.

1992: Re-elected to Senate.

1994: Elected Senate majority leader.

1995: Announces third bid for GOP presidential nomination.

1996: Wins enough primaries to assure nomination; resigns from Senate.

1920
1925
1930
1935
1940
1945
1950
1955
1960
1965
1970
1975
1980
1985
1990
1995

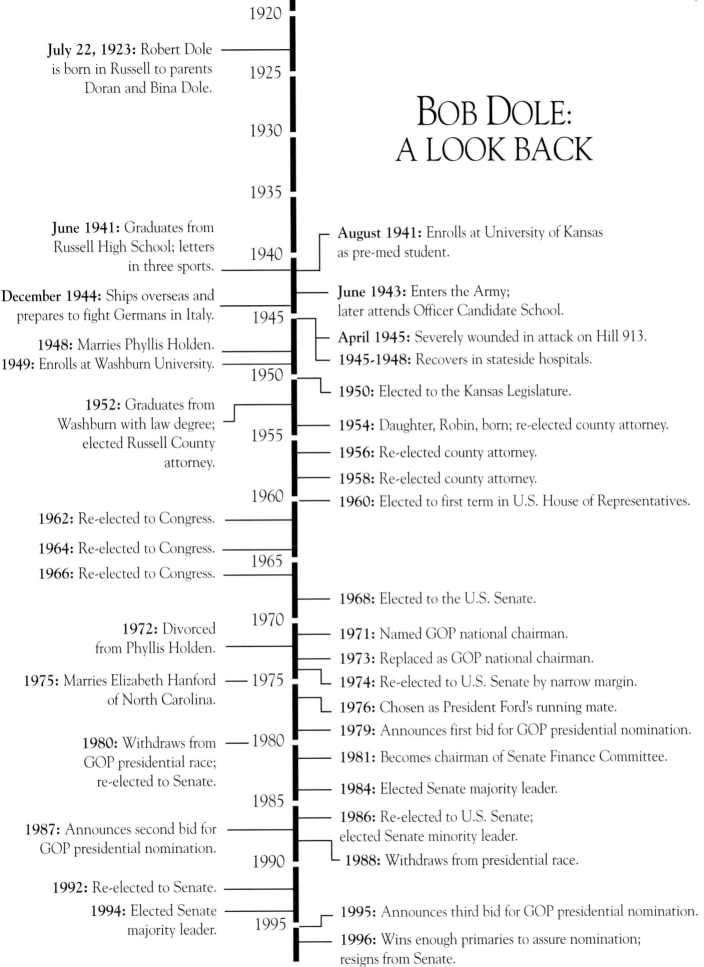

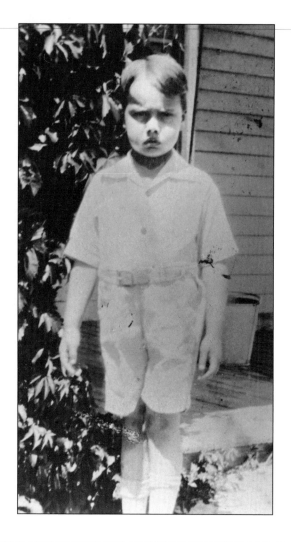

Doran and Bina Dole lived in a two-room frame house in Russell when their second child, Robert, was born in 1923. The home reflected the hard economic times of the Great Depression and Dust Bowl years. Life was simple, but a hayrack ride was fun and so was a spin for Bob and his younger brother, Kenny, in their father's 1927 Whippet.

"If you work hard and believe in what you're doing, it doesn't make much difference where you're from."

– Bob Dole

Doran Dole cared for his family with income from a small cream, egg and produce business. His habit of working late into the night hours formed a pattern his son would follow. His wife, Bina, sold Singer sewing machines to help support their four children: Kenny, Bob (back row on facing page), Norma Jean and Gloria. All but Norma Jean were on hand to carry rabbits home from a hunt.

"They all liked
homemade ice cream
and ate copious
amounts of it."

*– Russell Townsley, former
editor and publisher of the
Russell Daily News*

"Bina's specialty was fixing popcorn balls at Christmastime for all the children."

– *Lillian Papay, family friend*

Townspeople recall Doran always wearing overalls to work. His wife wanted him to look nice, so she made sure he had a clean pair to wear every day. Russell honored Doran, a volunteer firefighter for 50 years, by putting his name on the city's fire truck. He died in Washington, D.C., in 1975. Bina died in a Wichita, Kan., hospital in 1983. The four children model the latest swimwear, opposite page, and carry on under the tree on Christmas morning.

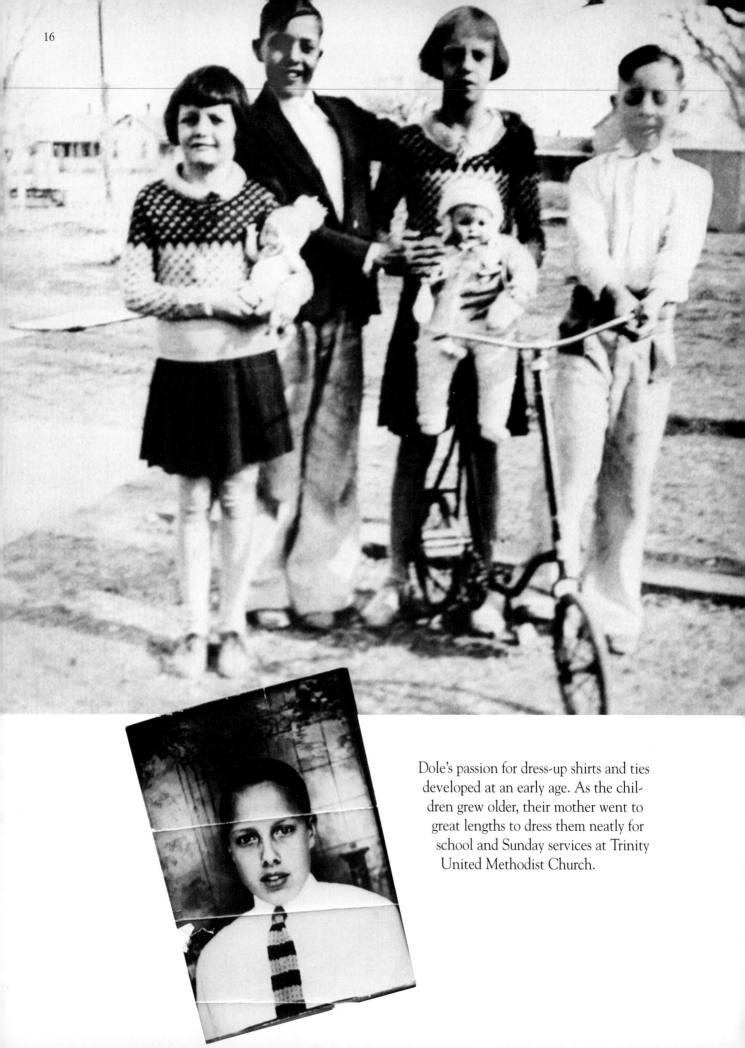

Dole's passion for dress-up shirts and ties developed at an early age. As the children grew older, their mother went to great lengths to dress them neatly for school and Sunday services at Trinity United Methodist Church.

School days were happy days at Simpson Elementary School in Russell, where Dole posed for a class picture in the fourth grade. By the time he was in junior high, facing page, Dole was slimming down and sprouting up.

The competition in sports appealed to Dole, who lettered three years in football, basketball and track. He was captain of the basketball team during his senior year at Russell High School and was selected for the Union Pacific All-Star team. At right, Phillip Ruppenthal and Dole in sweat suits after a track warm-up. The basketball lineup, facing page, included Ralph Resley, left, Dole and W.A. "Mick" Michaelis.

"His teammates said
Dole would never,
ever think of
breaking a
training rule in
high school."

— *Allan Evans, Russell
News/Record editor and publisher*

"Bud Smith, who was killed in the war, and Bob Dole were models in a fashion show about '39-'40. They were a couple dandies. Bob was so good-looking."

– Ken Holzer, Russell

At Dawson's drugstore in Russell, Dole (at left with G.B. "Bub" Dawson, above) and the Dawson brothers delighted customers who came to hear their sarcastic barbs and put-down humor. Some say Dole acquired his knack for quick one-liners there. His good looks earned him a spot in high school fashion shows, right.

****

Everytime Bob Dole even so much as acted as if he was going to shoot in the Cadet game, one of the Cadets would holler "Swish!!"

****

Sports Hash

There's nothing like the big city. **John Lowell Hogue** and **Bob Dole** kept running up to the fourth floor of their hotel in Newton just to ride down on the elevator.

****

Dole captured his share of attention in the Pony Express, the Russell High School newspaper.

****

Bob Dole, the Sampson of R. H. S., struts out out to football practice without pads. Some man, eh girls?

****

Dopey Thru' Out

Have you heard about **Bob Dole's** little brother, Kenny, beating him in the art of learning to dance? Why oh why can't someone persuade Bob to learn how, for if he is as smooth on the dance floor as he is on the basketball court, he should be a regular Astaire . . . .

HOGUE

DOLE

A late-game touchdown pass from quarterback Johnny Hogue to receiver Bob Dole wins the game against the Ellis Railroaders. Dole poses for a football team photo in 1940, when the Russell Broncos won their league championship with an undefeated season. Every member of that team went into the armed forces within the next three years.

Russell High School boasted four handsome young men as captains of its sports teams; the quartet earned the nickname of "The Four Horsemen." Clockwise from bottom left are: Phillip Ruppenthal, football; Lawrence Marsh, track; Bernard Smith, tennis; and Dole, basketball. Below, Dole is in the center of his journalism classroom photo. He was a shy but popular student in high school. On the facing page, Dole, left, poses with two of his best friends, Bud Smith, center, and Leon Mai, for a "mug shot" before cruising Russell.

"Most girls preferred a brunette, while only three girls preferred redheads. When asked if they wished boys to use scented soap, they answered, 'Yes, it would be sweet of them.'"

— *The Russell High School Pony Express, 1941*

Dole, with sisters Gloria and Norma Jean (in back), was the only one of the four Dole children to complete college. He entered KU as a pre-med student, but his injuries shifted him to law school after the war. He graduated magna cum laude from Washburn University Law School in Topeka, Kan., in 1952.

"Bob always was a bit different from others. He always tried a bit harder."
— *Russell Townsley*

Four members of his senior class of 1941 gather on Dole's front porch at 11th and Maple in Russell. Ready for a dressy outing are, from left, Leon Mai, Dole, Eddie Manweiler and Harold Bangerter.

At KU in 1942, Dole, below right, pursued his first love in sports, track. On the outdoor track, he specialized in the 440- and 880-yard races. During his high school years, he ran every morning to build his endurance and strength. In Washington, he used a treadmill.

"When I was 18, 19, 20, my primary interest was how fast I could run and how well I could do out on the basketball floor — whether I could catch a football. That seemed to be the greatest goal in life." — *Dole in 1976*

KAPPA SIGMA

Pledge activities drew Dole into the Kappa Sigma fraternity at the University of Kansas. In 1970, two years after he was elected to the U.S. Senate, Dole was named Kappa Sigma's Man of the Year, joining such other notables over the years as Senators Estes Kefauver and John Tower, newsmen Lowell Thomas and Edward R. Murrow, pianist/composer Hoagy Carmichael and famed heart surgeon Denton Cooley.

The cover of the 1942 Jayhawker shows a student reading a draft registration form. Publisher Allan Evans, attending KU at the same time as Dole, said the Army was advising men to stay in college because of a need for qualified officer candidates. Dole would not heed that advice. At left, he visits his grandfather's farm in Russell shortly before entering the army.

THE RUSSELL RECORD

RUSSELL KANSAS, MONDAY, DECEMBER 8, 1941

SEVERAL RUSSELL BOYS IN JAPANESE WAR ZONE

Announcement of Japan's Attack On Honolulu and Philippine Islands Shocks the World

Local affairs and the approaching Christmas season faded into the background yesterday when the news was flashed across the nation that Japan had declared war on the United States.

As elsewhere in the nation Russell was electrified with the announcement. Around radios in drug stores and places open for regular Sunday business hovered groups of people whose general concensus of opinion was "It sounds awful—the United States is really at war now."

As news of the history-making crisis was unfolded by constant radio announcements the importance of the day was registered by men and women up and down Main street.

In the far eastern war Russell county already has several young men in the army and navy forces whose parents today view events with grave concern.

... is Darold Thoman, son of Mr. and Mrs. Roy ... in Russell a month ago on a short navy ...lu. He was returned there ...weeks ago yester-

Beck, and
before his
Manila in the

DREAM THEATRE NEWS PRESENTS
"WAR WITH JAPAN"

Without declaration of war, Japan suddenly strikes – bombing Hawaii and other U. S. bases. The president takes prompt action! Congress declares war, with speed.

TODAY TOMORRO   **DREAM THEATRE**

ALSO WEDNESDAY · THURSDAY & FRIDAY

"The battlefield brings out a man's character and sensitivity. … You see into men's souls."

— *Dole in 1987*

Dole cut a dashing figure as a second lieutenant fresh out of Officer Candidate School in 1944. Although many of Dole's classmates, and his brother, Kenny, were sent to the Pacific theater of war, Dole was destined to fight in Europe. By December of that year, he had been sent to Italy, where it appeared the war might end before he saw action. He was severely wounded on April 14, 1945.

Dole had hoped to serve in the Medical Corps as his father had in World War I, but he found himself taking engineering and anti-tank gunnery training before going overseas to be a combat platoon leader.

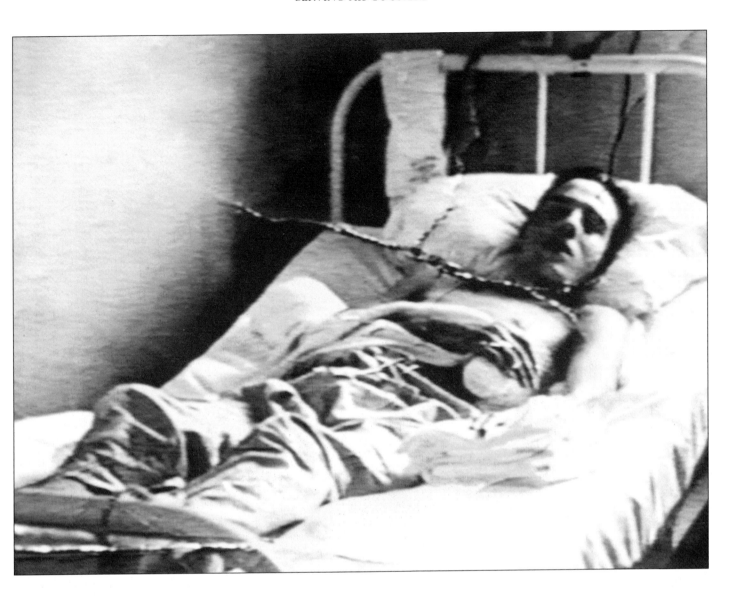

**WESTERN -
UNION** (09)

AJ2 64 GOVT=WASHINGTON DC 3 1247A

DORAN R DOLE=

1035 MAPLE RS=

THE SECRETARY OF WAR DESIRES ME TO EXPRESS HIS DEEP REGRET
THAT YOUR SON 2LT DOLE ROBERT J WAS SERIOUSLY WOUNDED IN
ITALY 14 APRIL 1945 PERIOD HOSPITAL SENDING YOU NEW ADDRESS
AND FURTHER INFORMATION PERIOD UNLESS SUCH NEW ADDRESS IS
RECEIVED ADDRESS MAIL FOR HIM QUOTE RANK NAME SERIAL
NUMBER (HOSPITALIZED) 2628 HOSPITAL SECTION APO 698 C/O
POSTMASTER NEW YORK NEW YORK UNQUOTE=

J A ULIO THE ADJUTANT GENERAL.

2LT 14 1945 2628 APO 698 C/O

Only weeks before the war in Europe ended, Dole was cut down by fierce German gunfire in northern Italy. His right shoulder shattered, he was shipped back to the states to spend most of the next 3 years in veterans' hospitals.

His mother and the family dogs showered Dole with therapeutic love and comfort during his long convalescence. Despite the damage to his athletic body, Dole never gave up. He only changed course.

"I remember how Bob liked to play 'Laughing on the Outside, Crying on the Inside' on the jukebox when he came home."

— *Chet Dawson, Russell druggist*

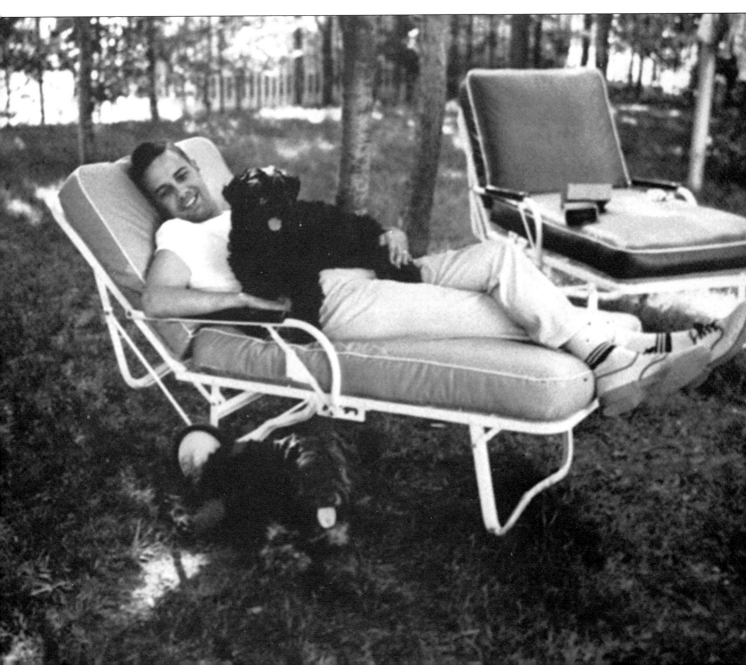

"Life becomes
learning
how to use
what you
have left."

— *Bob Dole*

Friends and family believe Dole's recovery from his war injuries and his rise to national political leadership were nothing short of a miracle. He is not a quitter, but he admitted to dark moments when he wondered, "Why me?"

"Mom used to have me go out in the back yard to ask him to come inside. She'd say: 'Tell him ten more minutes, dinner'll be ready.' He just worked so hard. He didn't want to quit."

— *Dole's sister Norma Jean Steele*

"A friend told me last year (1995) that Washburn didn't have a picture of Bob Dole. So I had this one enlarged and sent it to the dean of the law school with a note saying that for the guy at the right on the top row, this was probably his first election, and for the guy in the middle on the bottom row, it was his last election."   — *Retired U.S. District Judge Patrick F. Kelly*

After recovering from his war injuries, Dole enrolled at Washburn University in Topeka, where he earned a bachelor of arts degree and a law degree in 1952. He was one of the officers of the new Washburn Bar Association formed in 1949. The officers were, clockwise from top left, Bob Baker, vice president; Wayne Stallard, president; Dole, treasurer; Clyde Christy, bailiff; Pat Kelly, secretary; and Dick Cottle, student representative.

Caps and gowns and Washburn law degrees brought smiles from William J. Miller Jr., later president of Security Benefit Association in Topeka; State Rep. Bob Dole; and Sam Crow, who became a U.S. District Court judge. Dole was listed among 1951-52 selections of Who's Who in American Colleges and Universities.

Who's Who

IN AMERICAN COLLEGES AND UNIVERSITIES

Twenty-one Washburn University students were selected to be listed in the 1951-52 publication of WHO'S WHO AMONG STUDENTS IN AMERICAN UNIVERSITIES AND COLLEGES. They were chosen on the basis of points accumulated for participation in activities, leadership, service, and scholarship.

During the 17 years of organization, over 600 institutions have cooperated in selecting outstanding students for the honor. When chosen, the student receives a certificate from the Who's Who organization, recognition in the annual publication, and benefits of the Student Placement Service in finding a position.

Richard Hill, Jr., is not pictured.

Doris Baker   Peggy Codby Beatty   Jeanne Bowman

Elwin Cabbage

Robert Dole

John Egner

Joan Hardman   A. C. Herrick

George W. Otto   Lor

Elie

Compliments of

COTT~PUFFER
CHEVROLET

Phyllis Holden, a therapist who met Dole in a Michigan hospital, married him in 1948. She took part in his campaigns for Russell County attorney but loathed the pressure politics of Washington after Dole was elected to the Senate. The marriage ended in 1972. They had one child, Robin, who attracted smiles from her parents at her baptismal ceremony in 1954. Dole, soon to be elected to his second term as county attorney, sometimes wore glasses. Holding Robin is Phyllis Dole; looking on are Dole's mother, Bina, at rear between the parents; Phyllis' mother, Estelle Holden; and Jane Townsley, wife of Russell publisher Russell Townsley. Robin now lives in Virginia and is a frequent campaigner with her father. Her mother lives in Topeka and is married to a high school boyfriend from New Hampshire. A playful Robin, at right and on facing page, makes the most of precious time with her father.

After Dole was elected to Congress, and especially during his years in the Senate, trips back home, such as a visit with his father, above, stretched farther apart.

"Bob gets a lot of strength from within the walls of the family home."

— *Dole's sister Gloria Nelson*

"Kenny got us out of bed by honking his horn until we answered the door. He wouldn't let us dress up. We had to come as we were."

— G.B. "Bub" Dawson, *about wearing bathrobes to a New Year's Eve party*

At the party are: standing, Bub Dawson and his wife, Donna; back row, Betty Boxberger, Dottie Dole (Kenny's first wife), Harlan Boxberger, Gloria Nelson and Bob Dole; front row, Kenny Dole, Phyllis Dole and Jane Townsley. At right, Doran Dole wipes off a paintbrush as the Dole home gets a new coat of paint in 1955.

Dole is at left in the back row at a swearing-in ceremony, after he was re-elected as Russell County attorney in 1954.

"I lived in Osborne, 46 miles from Russell, and came over (to Russell) for ice cream in the daytime, but we stayed away at night — too wild, what with the oil boom and Walker Air Force Base west of town. We used to call it Little Chicago. The mores of the people were already changing by the time Dole as county attorney helped straighten things out."

— *Former Russell Police Chief Bob Tyler*

County Attorney Bob Dole dictates to secretary Wilma Tittel in his Russell Courthouse office in 1955. Dole, with glasses (facing page), gets ready to join a political caravan in Russell in 1952.

"If you don't get a lump in your throat when you drive through Russell, Kansas … then you've been away too long."

— *Dole in 1987*

ROBERT J. DOLE

Dole Is Installed As Kiwanis Head

New Officers for Year Assume Their Duties

New officers of the Kiwanis Club were installed today at the weekly luncheon of the civic club. They will serve a year.

County Attorney Robert J. Dole was installed as president. He succeeded Dr. A. D. Glenn who has held the post the past year

NORBERT DREILING, Hays, new lieutenant-governor for Division 9, installed the officers. Dreiling succeeded Roger Williams, Russell, as lieutenant governor.

Other local officers: Vice-president, Eugene Steinle; secretary, Calvin Haworth; and treasurer, Gene Dickerson. Dole had been vice-president, Paul Laubhan had served as treasurer, and Haworth succeeded himself as secretary.

the club's board

Dole was active in community and veterans' organizations before he left Russell for Washington. In a unique 1956 photo, facing page, Dole visits with two members of Congress he would replace in years to come: Congressman Wint Smith, left, whose retirement in 1960 led to Dole's winning his seat, and U.S. Sen. Frank Carlson, who would retire in 1968, allowing Dole to move into his seat after winning a primary contest with former Kansas Gov. William H. Avery and a general election race with Wichita lawyer William I. Robinson.

"There's nothing wrong with being a conservative. It's not like robbing a bank."

— *Dole, who supported Rep. Robert Taft of Ohio for vice president in 1964*

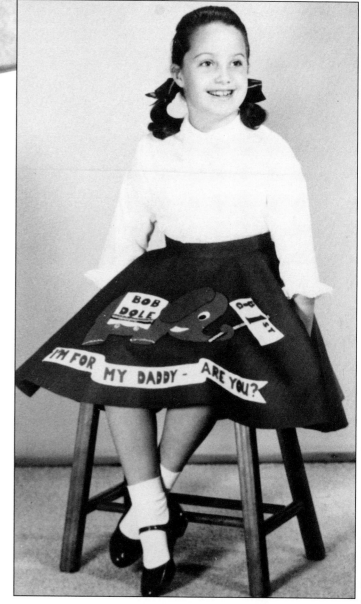

"You think of all the fun you have in politics, all the people you have met and all the people who have done something for you and never asked anything in return except for you to be a good representative … that's really what it's all about."

— *Dole in 1987*

President Eisenhower gave Dole a helping hand in his first campaign for Congress in 1960. Dole dropped the R.J. initials (for Robert Joseph) after his early congressional campaigns. Russell area women formed a Dolls for Dole team to boost his candidacy and passed out a lot of Dole pineapple juice at campaign stops.

In 1963, Dole posed with his parents on the steps of the Capitol. He checks notes, below, with Shirley Temple Black. Throughout his eight years in the U.S. House of Representatives, Dole's votes reflected the conservative philosophy of his western Kansas constituents. Although he voted for the Civil Rights Act of 1964 and the Voting Rights Act of 1965, he opposed much of the social legislation proposed by Presidents Kennedy and Johnson. He answered his critics by telling them,

"Once we forget where we're from, we're finished."

Dole Proposes 'Day of Bread'

WASHINGTON — President Nixon was asked today to proclaim an annual "Day of Bread" during a "Harvest Festival" in observance in late October.

Sen. Bob Dole, R-Kan., introduced a resolution, noting that "Wheat and specifically, bread, has become especially important in the growing worldwide concern with assuring adequate and nutritious diets for all men, women and children at home and abroad."

Cosponsors of the measure included Sens. James Pearson, R-Kan.; Fred Harris, D-Okla.; Roman Hruska, R-Neb.

Dole said it...

Once elected to Congress, Dole wasted little time getting involved in presidential politics. He is between Sen. Barry Goldwater of Arizona and Rep. William E. Miller of New York above and at right; at left in the top photo is GOP national chairman Dean Burch. Goldwater and Miller formed the GOP presidential ticket in 1964. On the facing page, young Russellites get ready to pour Dole pineapple juice at a campaign event for Dole's Senate race in 1968. In his early years in the Senate, Dole used quick-response counterattacks against Democratic criticism of President Nixon's administration. For this he was dubbed the "Dole Patrol."

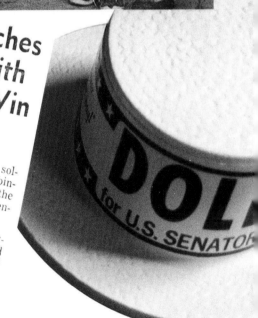

"He's the first man we've had around here for a long time who will grab the other side by the hair and drag them down the hill."

— *Sen. Barry Goldwater*

Dole Reaches Senate With Crushing Win

By LYNNE HOLT
Eagle Political Writer

Republican Bob Dole has solidly crushed William I. Robinson's 1968 hopes to spend the next six years in the U.S. Senate.

U.S. Rep. Dole, 45, now serving the 1st District, grabbed and maintained a commanding lead Tuesday in his bid for the Senate.

With 1,751 of the 2,906 precincts reporting Dole had 295,390 votes (61 per cent) against 188,181 votes (39 per cent) for Robinson.

Among Dole's winning areas was Sedgwick County where he received 12 per cent more of the vote than did Robinson — in Robinson's home territory.

Senate nominee Dole huddles with the Rev. Billy Graham and U.S. Sen. Frank Carlson at the 1968 Republican National Convention in Miami Beach. Graham, a close friend of Carlson, was there to hear Carlson nominated as a favorite-son candidate for president. Carlson was winding up a 40-year career in public office. Right, Dole is welcomed to the convention by Kansas delegates. On the opposite page, Dole is flanked by presidential nominee Richard Nixon, Michigan Gov. George Romney and U.S. Sen. Strom Thurmond.

"I want to introduce the man who yesterday won the U.S. Senate nomination, receiving 70 percent of the Republican votes cast."

— *McDill "Huck" Boyd, about Dole at 1968 convention*

Unsuccessful GOP presidential candidate Nelson Rockefeller shares a laugh with Kansas Congressmen Dole and Larry Winn at an October 1968 GOP meeting in Kansas. Rick Harman, GOP candidate for governor, is at left. Right, Dole enjoys a Kansas-Kansas State football game appearance with Alaska Gov. Walter Hickel, a former Kansan. Hickel later became President Nixon's secretary of the interior. Facing page, Dole listens as California Gov. Ronald Reagan speaks at a GOP meeting in Topeka. At Reagan's right is Rep. John Rhodes of Arizona, another former Kansan.

Robin Dole has been an active member of Dole's campaign teams since his first run for Congress in 1960 when she was 6 years old. When her father was the GOP national chairman, she attended her first national convention in 1972, serving as a page on the podium. She is a graduate of Virginia Polytechnic Institute. In 1975, she represented Kansas in the Cherry Blossom Festival in Washington.

"… As your chairman, loyalty to the president will be a primary concern. It will be proper. It will be unyielding. It will be continuous. The president has a right to expect (that) and he deserves as much."

— *Dole on assuming party chairmanship in 1971*

Dole Prepares To Take Reins Of GOP Today

By LYNNE HOLT
Eagle Political Writer

WASHINGTON — On the eve of his election Friday as the 46th Republican national chairman, Sen. Bob Dole was conducting himself like a senator from Kansas.

At least so

"I recall that during our first meeting, Dr. K administered the verbal equivalent of a slap in the face. He would do all he could, but there would be no miracles. 'The choice is all up to you,' he said."

— Bob Dole, speaking of Dr. Hampar Kelikian, the Chicago surgeon who helped him regain some use of his injured right arm through several operations beginning in 1947

Dole and his father, Doran (standing), talk with Kelikian and his wife during their visit to Russell.

Then California Gov. Ronald Reagan went to Wichita in 1974 to boost Dole in his tough Senate race with Democratic Congressman Bill Roy. Dole won that contest by less than 1 percent of the vote, the only time his re-election to the Senate was ever threatened.

Dole's marriage to Elizabeth Hanford, a member of the Federal Trade Commission, on Dec. 6, 1975, highlighted a relationship that rocketed them to one of Washington's most powerful couples. She has worked for six presidents, including a stint as secretary of transportation for President Reagan, and is on leave from her post as president of the American Red Cross. Dole's parents attended the Washington wedding, but his father died a few days later before they could return to Russell.

Dole, Hanford to Wed Tonight

From Our Washington Bureau

WASHINGTON — Senator Bob Dole and Federal Trade Commissioner Elizabeth Hanford will marry in a private ceremony tonight at the Bethlehem Chapel in Washington's Episcopal Cathedral.

Rev. Dr. Edward L. R. Elson, chaplain of the Senate, will perform the 6 p.m. marriage before family members at Washington Cathedral.

A large reception is planned following the wedding at the Washington Club in the "embassy row" area of the nation's capitol. From 500 to 600 guests, including members of Congress Cabinet officers, are invited to the reception.

It will be the first marriage for the commissioner, 39, and second for the Senator, 52.

A wedding breakfast will be hosted at 12:30 p.m. today by Asst. Defense Secretary and Mrs. Robert Ellsworth and Mr. and Mrs. John Van Hanford Jr.

Mrs. Hanford, a sister-in-law of the bride, will be the matron of honor at the wedding. Ellsworth, a former Kansas congressman, will serve as the Republican senator's best man.

"I will certainly continue with my post and don't expect that to create any problems. Bob works long hours, but then so do I, and our offices are only about two blocks apart. "

— *Elizabeth Hanford, shortly before her marriage to Dole*

"I am really thrilled with the opportunity of having Bob Dole as my running mate. Bob Dole has been a team player."

— *President Gerald Ford in Russell in 1976*

President Ford, Elizabeth Dole and Sen. Dole step out of Air Force One and wave to a crowd of well-wishers gathered at an airfield in Salina, Kan., on Aug. 20, 1976. This was their first appearance in the state after Ford picked Dole as his running mate at the Kansas City GOP convention. They took a 70-mile flight by helicopter to Russell for Dole's hometown welcome.

President Ford went to Russell because Dole had suggested that if he wanted to start his campaign in the heartland, "I know of a little town where we can start." Townspeople had less than 24 hours to get ready for the presidential visit. A crowd estimated at 6,000 packed the courthouse lawn and was fed hot dogs cooked on batteries of backyard grills. On the facing page, Russell area farmer Don Reinhardt and his son, Steve, plowed a large campaign sign in his wheat field for air passengers flying over the area in 1976.

"The time when I needed help … and the people of Russell helped. That was a long time ago, and I thank you for it again."

— *An emotional moment when Dole recalled how Russell people collected $1,800 in 1947 to pay his hospital bills to repair his injured arm*

"It's here somewhere, Mr. President."

— Dole's mother (above), embarrassed to keep President Ford waiting while she looked for the key to her home during his 1976 visit. It had been kicked aside from its usual hiding place.

From left are Ford, Dole, his mother (behind door) and Elizabeth Dole.

In January 1978, Dole returned to Russell for the dedication of a monument marking the site where the Ford-Dole team launched its campaign. "We were not successful. But neither were we really defeated … real defeat is when you accept failure," said Dole. From left are Nancy Lane, Bina Dole, the senator and Elizabeth Dole.

Sen. Dole emerges from a Russell voting booth in 1976 when he was a candidate for vice president. Below, he dons a strike hat given him by farmers threatening to strike if farm prices were not raised. At lower right, he chats with townspeople in the drugstore where he worked as a youth. A grim Dole, facing page, ponders a question from one of 500 farmers who mounted a tractorcade to Topeka in December 1977 to protest low farm prices.

"Farm legislation, good legislation, is at best difficult to get through an urban-dominated Congress. The real salvation for agriculture is market development, creating new outlets for what we raise and process."

— *Dole, when he first said he would seek appointment to the Senate Agriculture Committee in 1968*

"The liberals who lost their seats are good people, but they're out of step with a majority of the American people."

— *Dole, following 1980 elections which gave the GOP a Senate majority*

Dole to Get Top GOP Job On Finance

By BETTY WELLS
Staff Writer

Kansas Sen. Bob Dole will become ranking Republican on the Senate Finance Committee during the next congressional session, sacrificing his ranking minority position on the Agriculture Committee.

The Finance committee is considered one of the most powerful Senate committees, and the move would give Dole more opportunity for national exposure should he enter the 1980 race for the GOP presidential nomination.

campaigning heavily around the country this

The senator's first campaign for the GOP presidential nomination failed to catch on with the public in 1979-80. With his wife at his side, Dole campaigned in Iowa, where the news media drew attention to his poorly organized and poorly financed effort. He easily won re-election to the Senate and assumed chairmanship of the powerful Senate Finance Committee when Republicans gained control of the upper house.

The Dole children — Kenny, Norma Jean, Bob and Gloria — relax at a family gathering in Russell for their mother's 80th birthday in 1983. She died five months later in a Wichita hospital. Kenny Dole died in 1993.

Proud of her son's achievements, Bina Dole is taken, facing page, to a Russell appearance in an antique car driven by newspaper publisher Russell Townsley with his wife, Jane, in the passenger seat.

DOLE GETS FAVOR — President Reagan, in an expansive mood after his big victory in the tax-cut battle, called a number of key congressmen and senators to thank them for their support.

When he talked to Kansas Sen. Bob Dole, Reagan asked if there was something he could do for him. Dole told him he could make a phone call to his mother, who was in a Russell hospital at the time, because he was sure it would cheer her up.

Imagine the surprise when Bina Dole picked up the jangling phone in her room and heard the president of the United States wishing her well.

They talked for several minutes. Reagan told Dole's mother how much he appreciated her son's help on the tax cut. Mrs. Dole told the president of seeing Nancy Reagan on the televised wedding ceremony of Great Britain's Prince Charles and Lady Diana.

Mrs. Doran Dole
Mother of Russell County's
Most Famous Son
Vice-Presidential Candidate
BOB DOLE

Family Members Recall Memories Of Bina Dole

By Al Polczinski
Staff Writer

RUSSELL — A funeral, said the Rev. Rick Thornton, has a way of bringing people together to share the gift of memories of someone special.

Anyone could tell that Bina Dole the woman who lay in the silver-trimmed deep blue casket at the front of the Trinity United Methodist Church, was someone special. She died Monday in Wichita at the age of 80.

AMONG THE banks of floral tributes flanking the coffin were cards from President and Nancy Reagan, the staff of the Senate Finance Committee, Heidi Berenson of the Good Morning America television crew, the Topeka Federation of Labor and the Kansas Bankers Association.

"You have to try to help your children."

— *Bina Dole, about her campaign work for the senator. She always worried whether he ate right and just knew he didn't.*

• • •

A Dole for a Dole — Another of Kansas Sen. Bob Dole's famous one-liners made a big hit with his home state delegation Monday.

Because Elizabeth Dole was ill with a cold, the senator said, he subbed for her at a Nieman Marcus reception in her honor.

"I didn't look too good in a dress, but some didn't know the difference," he said.

• • •

"Only two? I thought we hired three."
— *Dole on spying two protesters outside a Wichita hotel*

By the time Sen. Dole accepted the Republican leadership role in 1984, he had gained a reputation as an arbitrator, a tough negotiator, in building a consensus to support a proposed solution to a crisis. He was a key player in Social Security reforms, the 1985 farm bill, aid for the handicapped and various tax and spending measures.

"Service is in my blood. We love politics or we wouldn't be here."

— Dole, with his wife at an informal luncheon with President Reagan and senior presidential aide James Baker

Travelers on Interstate 70 know where they are when they reach Russell. Large signs at both ends of town welcome them to "Bob Dole Country."

"When I look out on Main Street … I see the faces of people who know me best … people who have always accepted me and believed in me." — *Dole in 1987*

In time for his second run at the presidency, Dole and his wife collaborated on a book about their lives and busy careers. It was a story, they said, about two people who love their work second only to each other.

"No doubt about it, the people of Russell made a big difference in my life. I would like to give something back — not only for my neighbors, but for all Americans."

— Bob Dole in "Unlimited Partners" and as he announced for the presidency in 1987

A downcast Dole, silhouetted against a stage curtain, seemed to sense minutes before he was told that he would not be George Bush's choice for vice president on the 1988 Republican ticket. Kansans at the convention expressed mixed feelings; they didn't want to lose Dole in the Senate but thought he was the most experienced person Bush could select.

"I am ready and eager to serve as George Bush's 'point man' in a Republican-controlled Senate come January."

— *Dole in 1988 convention speech*

"Like everybody else, I get frustrated and tired sometimes. You have to play the hand that's dealt."

— *Dole in 1983*

Instead of moving into the White House in 1989 as they had hoped, Dole and his wife, Elizabeth, were all smiles as they continued their action-packed lives from their Watergate apartment. Dole continued to be minority leader in the Senate, where he had time to play with his dog, Leader. Elizabeth looked around for another job, finding what she wanted as president of the American Red Cross. The doormat is still out at the Dole home in Russell.

"He (Dole) has been a tireless champion of individuals with physical, mental and developmental disabilities and is recognized as their most forceful public spokesman."

— *Gene A. Budig, former KU chancellor*

ROBERT J. DOLE
HUMAN DEVELOPMENT
CENTER
DEDICATED
AUGUST 25, 1990
ROBERT A. CREIGHTON, CHAIRMAN
KANSAS BOARD OF REGENTS
GENE A. BUDIG, CHANCELLOR
THE UNIVERSITY OF KANSAS

In 1988, the University of Kansas announced plans to build the $12 million Robert J. Dole Human Development Center, which opened in 1990. Its programs seek to answer the needs of the disabled through education, rehabilitation and treatment. Below, Dole checks a bust of himself. With him is Armenian sculptor Friedrich M. Sogojan, who presented the bust as a gift from the people of Armenia to Dole for his efforts to aid victims of a 1988 earthquake there.

A seemingly endless stream of natural disasters — floods, hurricanes and tornadoes — has inundated the American Red Cross during the time Elizabeth Dole has been its president. At left, she greets former first lady Nancy Reagan during one of Dole's many nation-hopping trips. Above, she picks her way through debris strewn throughout the Golden Spur Mobile Home Park in Andover, Kan., by the devastating tornado of April 26, 1991.

"This is as bad as a war zone. The Red Cross will be around as long as there is a need."

— *Elizabeth Dole following her inspection of the Andover tornado site*

Playing host to visiting dignitaries and celebrities of all kinds is part of a Senate leader's duties. Below, Yasser Arafat, chairman of the Palestine Liberation Organization, talks business at a breakfast with Senate leaders Bob Dole, left, and George Mitchell. Lifting a ban on financial assistance to PLO-connected groups was a prime item of this discussion. At right, Dole spends time with Prince Andrew and Miss America Heather Whitestone during their Washington visits.

"I was there and witnessed the emotion as memories came flooding back, memories of heroism, the sacrifices, the pain men and women suffered."

— *Sen. Bob Dole as he and Elizabeth (opposite page) were in Normandy in June 1994 for the 50th anniversary of the D-Day invasion*

"I believe that history has validated Richard Nixon's vision. That is why leaders from Washington, from Moscow to Beijing, to London, to New York, seek his counsel and wisdom."

— Dole in June 1992

Former President Richard Nixon autographs one of his books, "Seize the Moment: America's Challenge in a One-Superpower World," during a Wichita visit in June 1992 to help Dole in his Senate re-election campaign. Dole admired Nixon's stewardship of the nation's foreign policy and tried to help rebuild Nixon's image, tarnished by the Watergate scandal that led to his resignation in August 1974.

"They wanted his protection in a dangerous world. These were the people from whom he had come and who have come to Yorba Linda (Calif.) these past few days by the tens of thousands, no longer silent in their grief."

— Dole in his eulogy at President Nixon's funeral on April 27, 1994

The volatile relationship between Israel and its Mideast neighbors is always a hot topic on Capitol Hill. Below, Senate Majority Leader Bob Dole and Majority Whip Trent Lott, who was elected majority leader after Dole resigned from the Senate, discuss the area's problems with Shimon Peres, prime minister of Israel. Another divisive issue — farm legislation — brings Agriculture Secretary Dan Glickman, above left, to Dole's office to check a vote tally. Once bitter primary foes, Dole and President George Bush find common ground for a cordial meeting. Dole was one of Bush's strongest supporters in the Senate.

"We cannot. We must not let that happen this time."
— First lady Hillary Rodham Clinton at Midwest Health Care Summit in Kansas City, Mo., after noting that other presidents had tried but failed to pass health reforms

Sen. Bob Dole contemplates a point made by the first lady in her address to the health care summit in Kansas City in 1993. Later, at another health reform meeting in Garden City, Kan., Dole said the Clinton Administration plan would increase employer costs and could lead to a loss of jobs.

A B-2 Stealth bomber looms in the background as Dole speaks to a crowd at McConnell Air Force Base in Wichita for the christening of the plane "The Spirit of Kansas" on May 13, 1996. The senator played a key role in securing federal funding for rebuilding base installations destroyed by a tornado in 1991.

"I worry about our defense. I know there are a lot of very talented people here who are going to continue to do that. ... I would hope that we would keep in mind there are still threats around the world." — *Dole in his farewell speech to the Senate on June 11, 1996.*

After a rocky beginning to their relationship in 1994, House Speaker Newt Gingrich and Senate Majority Leader Bob Dole learned to work together. They share a laugh even though the national debt clock is nearing $5 trillion. Dole addressed the nation's debt and budget deficit as two of the government's most difficult problems. In his presidential campaign announcement speech in 1995, he proposed abolishing four federal departments — Housing and Urban Development, Education, Energy and Commerce — saying these matters are best left in the hands of the states.

"As a young man in a small town, my parents taught me to put my trust in God, not government, and never confuse the two."

— Dole on April 10, 1995

Dole and his wife, Elizabeth, react to a
rousing welcome from a large crowd in
Topeka's ExpoCentre on their arrival for his
announcement of his candidacy for president
on April 10, 1995. Gov. Bill Graves and his
wife, Linda, lend their support to the third bid
by their state's favorite-son candidate.
From Topeka, the Doles began a 10-state
announcement trip that ended four days later
with a hometown reception in Russell.

"And so today, tempered by adversity, seasoned by experience, mindful of the world as it is yet confident it can be made better, I have come home to Kansas with a grateful heart to declare I am a candidate for the presidency of the United States."   — *Dole in Russell, April 14, 1995*

Sen. Dole displayed an abiding interest in the concerns of the elderly, as in this recent visit to his hometown.

"… One of the stories Bob Dole likes to tell in speeches and interviews has to do with the events in the first two weeks of 1983 when, quite literally, the Social Security system was saved. … The only part of the tale he leaves out is his own role. It could not have happened without him. To the contrary, he made it happen. I was there. I so attest."   *— Sen. Patrick Moynihan, D-N.Y., in a farewell tribute to Dole, June 11, 1996*

Two hometown boys make it back to Russell, occasionally together. Sen. Arlen Specter of Pennsylvania waves to Russell folks as he and Dole perch atop the city fire truck named for Dole's father, who was a volunteer firefighter for more than 50 years. Specter, born in Wichita in 1930, moved to Russell in 1942, the year after Dole graduated from high school. He graduated there in 1947. Specter ran against Dole for the Republican presidential nomination briefly in 1995 but withdrew after failing to excite many primary voters.

Dole was talking at a Johnston, Iowa, rally for him in the high school gymnasium on Jan. 13, 1996, when he spied a familiar face in the crowd. A smile crosses his face as he recognizes Ralph Resley, a classmate and teammate from his Russell High School days. Resley was there to visit his daughter, Linda Scott, who grew up in Russell and lives in Johnston. Minutes later, Dole left for a debate in nearby Des Moines with other Republican presidential candidates prior to the Iowa caucuses where Dole won his first major contest in 1996.

"Ralph, what are you doing here?"

— *Dole, as he came over to shake hands with Resley at the Johnston rally*

"... My time to leave this office has come, and I will seek the presidency with nothing to fall back on but the judgment of the people, and nowhere to go but the White House or home."
— *Dole, on May 15, 1996, announcing he would resign his Senate seat and majority leadership post on or about June 11, 1996*

Elizabeth Dole gives her husband a hug after his announcement that he would leave the Senate to devote full time to his campaign for president. She understood his reluctance to forgo the exposure his leadership duties brought him but agreed that those duties required too much of his time.

LEAVING THE U.S. SENATE

Bob Dole's resignation from the U.S. Senate on June 11,
1996, prompted an outpouring of tributes from his Senate
colleagues of both parties. They praised his leadership, his
ability to build consensus and the bank-on-it value of his
word. Among the tributes, one theme was central:
Dole's values, work ethic and leadership traits had been
shaped in and by Russell, Kansas. Here are some excerpts
from his colleagues' remarks.

"… Senator Dole and I both grew up in Russell, Kansas.
I moved to Russell from Wichita when I was 12 years old,
so I have known Senator Dole for a good many years.
My father, Harry Specter, was a friend of his father,
Doran Dole. My dad was in the junk business, and the only
scale big enough at the time to weigh the junkyard truck was
the Dole scale and elevator run by Bob Dole's father.
" … Both the Doles and the Specters, figuratively,
lived on the wrong side of the tracks. It is a true story that
the Dole family, during the Depression, moved out of the first
floor of their home to live in the basement to help defray
expenses at a very tough time when Kansas was a dust bowl.
Bob Dole grew up and worked at Dawson Drugs at the soda
fountain. There is sort of a legendary
and famous story about how he would flip the ice cream and
catch it behind his back. I recounted that story not long ago
on a campaign appearance for the presidency in Delaware
County. Bob added that sometimes when the ice cream fell
to the floor, it became a chocolate shake.
"He went to college, a tough thing to do in the early 1940s.
Russell High School had the state debating championship,
but Bob Dole chose not to be a debater. He was a renowned
high school athlete. And then we all know of his heroics during World War II and of his injuries and how he laid his life
on the line. He did not suffer loss of life but did suffer loss of
limb, and came back with a phenomenal rehabilitation."

— *Sen. Arlen Specter, Pennsylvania*

"I have to say something here that I am sure Bob Dole does not
know, but I am going to say it publicly because it means so
much to me. My brother died shortly before Bob Dole got
wounded in the Second World War. My brother was very dear
to me. I was only 10 years old when he died. When we received
the news, I immediately got a white streak of hair on the right
side of my forehead because it was such a shock to me.
"He was killed in the Ploiesti oil raid, which, of course, was

the pivotal oil raid of the European war because it knocked
out all of the Vienna-Austrian oilfields that Hitler depended
on. But Jess' death was a tremendous shock to us.
   "When I came to the Senate, Bob Dole put his
arm around me. He looked like my brother, to a large degree.
My brother had the same color hair, was about the same
height, about the same build. My brother was a football
player as well. He looked a lot like my brother. I have always
considered Bob Dole, for good or bad, to be my brother."

— *Sen. Orrin Hatch, Utah*

   "The quote I like best comes from the story of the
1952 county attorney election itself. Two young men who
had come back from World War II were running — Bob
Dole and Dean Ostrum. Dean was a bright young man who
had enjoyed many of life's advantages and was the son of per-
haps the best lawyer in Russell. Bob Dole didn't have all the
advantages in life, had seen more adversity in 29 years than
most people see in a lifetime, and was the son of Doran Dole,
who worked in a local creamery. As the campaign wore on,
Bob outthought and outhustled his opponent, won by 200
votes and launched his political career.
   "The quote I like is from Dean Ostrum, years after
the campaign was over: 'How long was my day? I don't know,
but it wasn't as long as Bob Dole's, I'm sure of that.'
   "Forty-four years later that statement still rings true.
No one I know has ever outworked Bob Dole."

— *Sen. William Cohen, Maine*

   "The heartlands of the Kansas prairies are where Bob Dole
learned about being tough and not giving in when in the
same situation the average person might simply give up the
fight. While this is a region of simple beauty, kind people and
strong values, during the time of Bob Dole's youth it was also
a place that was rife with hardships for those who lived there.
It was a place where hard work was not a virtue. It was a
necessity for survival, especially during the nation's most
severe economic crisis, the Great Depression.
   "In his hometown of Russell, Kansas, Bob Dole also learned
about things such as patriotism and a commitment to serving
the nation. He was taught that these words represented more
than mere ideas or ideals, they were part of the responsibili-
ties of citizenship in this great land."

— *Sen. Strom Thurmond, South Carolina*

So many last-minute things to attend to — placing a final call to House Speaker Newt Gingrich about Senate action, checking the packing up of his mementos from his elegant majority leader's offices for storage elsewhere, and one last look back, facing page, before he strides into the Capitol corridors a private citizen.

"… It has been a great ride. There have been a few bumps along the way." — *Dole in his farewell speech on June 11, 1996*

"... Bob Dole's steady presentation and his can-do attitude ... has helped the Senate through so many rough times."

— *Sen. Nancy Landon Kassebaum, R-Kan.,*
in her farewell tribute to Dole

"I always thought that differences were a healthy thing, and that is why we are all so healthy, because we have a lot of differences in this chamber. I have never seen a healthier group in my life." — *Dole in his farewell speech*

Hundreds of Capitol Hill workers of all ranks spill over the steps of the Capitol to give Sen. Bob Dole a Washington send-off. He ended a 35-year-long career in the House and Senate on June 11, 1996. This was a time for putting aside partisan differences and showing respect for a man who had influenced, if not directed, much of the work product of not only the Senate but also of Congress as a whole for nearly three decades.

"… America has been my life. And the very least
a presidential candidate owes America is his full attention,
everything he can give, everything he has — and that is what
America shall receive from me."
— *Dole, announcing his intention to resign from the Senate, May 15, 1996*